Stephanie

May words always
help you abolish borders

Like a Straw Bird It Follows Me
and Other Poems

Steve

Thank you for your

hospitality

[handwritten signature]

Like a Straw Bird
It Follows Me
and Other Poems

GHASSAN ZAQTAN

TRANSLATED FROM THE ARABIC

BY FADY JOUDAH

YALE UNIVERSITY PRESS ■ NEW HAVEN & LONDON

A MARGELLOS
WORLD REPUBLIC OF LETTERS BOOK

The Margellos World Republic of Letters is dedicated to making literary works from around the globe available in English through translation. It brings to the English-speaking world the work of leading poets, novelists, essayists, philosophers, and playwrights from Europe, Latin America, Africa, Asia, and the Middle East to stimulate international discourse and creative exchange.

Library of Congress Cataloging-in-Publication Data
Zaqtan, Ghassan.
[Ka-tayr min al-qashsh yatba'uni. English]
Like a straw bird it follows me and other poems / Ghassan Zaqtan ; translated from the Arabic by Fady Joudah.
    p.   cm. — (A Margellos world republic of letters book)
Includes bibliographical references.
ISBN 978-0-300-17316-1 (cloth : alk. paper)
I. Joudah, Fady, 1971–. II. Title.
PJ7876.A6565K3813 2012
892.7′16—dc23   2011026640

Yale University Press books may be purchased in quantity for educational, business, or promotional use. For information, please e-mail sales.press@yale.edu (U.S. office) or sales@yaleup.co.uk (U.K. office).

Set in Electra and Nobel types by Keystone Typesetting, Inc.
Printed in the United States of America.

A catalogue record for this book is available from the British Library.

This paper meets the requirements of ANSI/NISO Z39.48-1992 (Permanence of Paper).

10 9 8 7 6 5 4 3 2 1

CONTENTS

Translator's Preface   ix

Acknowledgments   xxi

FROM *Luring the Mountain* (1998)

    The Dead in the Garden   3

    Neighboring Sounds   4

    Additions to the Past   5

    Like One Who Waits for Me   6

    Not Yet   7

    A Regretful Young Jaheer Man   8

    The Song of the Drowned   10

    The Song of the Betrayed   11

    The Song of the First Patrol   12

    Just a Song   13

    The Horses' Hymn   14

    The Gambler's Hymn   15

    The Islands   16

    A Graphic 1994   20

    A Graphic 1995   22

    Salty Hills   23

    A Prophecy   25

FROM *Biography in Charcoal* (2003)

Black Horses   29

Wolves   31

Wolves, Also   33

An Enemy Comes Down the Hill   35

Biography in Charcoal   37

Four Sisters from Zakariyya   38

The Canyon   39

Preliminary Sketch   40

Amman 1966   41

Beirut, August 1982   42

A Carving   44

Ramallah 2000   45

The Camp Prostitute   47

A Going   49

A Horse   50

Like a Straw Bird It Follows Me (2008)

PRETEXTS

Remembering the Grandmother   55

Remembering the Lonely   56

Remembering the Repentant   57

The Orchard's Song   58

Song of the Orchard's Watchman   59

Song of the Orchard's Watchman and His Son   60

Remembering Fatima   61

The Absentee's Song   62

The Hoopoes Lead to Me   64

Follow the Well   65

This Is My Only Profession   66

The Bird Follows Me   69

Pretexts   70

Only Her Dream Will Tell of Her   71

What She Loved Is Hers and What I Saw Is Mine   72

A Small Hostel in Genoa   73

Remembering Silk   74

I Have a Reason Other Than This   75

Cavafy's Builders   76

Remembering Weeping   77

Remembering Sleep   78

ALONE AND THE RIVER BEFORE ME   79

THE STRANGER IN HIS ICON

Saba and Hijaz   91

Wood Carving   92

The Stranger in His Icon   94

Ancient Alleyways   95

Stephanie's Window   96

The One You Accidentally Found in the Mirror   97

A Picture of the House in Beit Jala   98

As if He Were She   100

You're Not Alone in the Wilderness   103

The Orchard of Roman Olives

Where She Used to Stand   107

The Springs   108

He Wasn't Sleeping   109

He Thought Long of Going Back There   110

The Orchard of Roman Olives   111

Like a Dream at Noon   112

Silent Nature   113

Everything as It Was   115

Notes   119

TRANSLATOR'S PREFACE

Since the publication of his important 1988 collection *The Heroism of Things*, and especially over the past ten years, Ghassan Zaqtan has been a welcome presence for many young Arab poets, Palestinian and otherwise. After 1967, in Palestine and across the Arab world, Zaqtan and a few other poets of his generation found themselves in the shadow of a poetry largely concerned with gathering identity fragments of the individual in a collective mode. And they began to look elsewhere. Zaqtan, through quiet lyric, focused on the palpable daily cares, the molecular details that proliferate and unravel as they proliferate, toward unknown destinations that cut vision down to size. "This is my only profession," he writes in a recent poem,

> to author a bend in the story
> so we can prolong the evening
> or make predictions
> and matters bearable.

Zaqtan consciously moved away from mythologizing exile and displacement and homed in on the poem as textural movements, visual and tactile, whose reservoir of everyday things became endless projections that sculpt (or crumble) sound and form. His poetry is replete with "lost things" that link up with each other and expand the maze. Various alleyways and corridors, windows and pots, bedsheets and letters, rooms and houses connect to routes of escape from loss and memory. What amasses is constant dissipation, a perfect mess, an entropy of information. He shuttles his poetry between prosody and free verse, and between the objectively pithy and the obsessively thorough, the austere and the lavish, as two faces of indeterminacy's coin. As a lyricist, within his ordinary and observational stance, Zaqtan is as intense as he is slack and disarming. A mutual intimacy of transmission, of contiguity, exists between him and his subjects, "gathering their sleeves from the corners of their seats / like a cold [he] gather[s] them."

Zaqtan is also a novelist, an editor, and a filmmaker. His acclaimed second novel in 1994, *Describing the Past*, illuminates his predilection for whirling inventories with which he has enhanced his poetry and transfigured his memory. The novel is a lyrical love story told from the standpoint of three characters in a swift tempo that manages a wealth of detail in fewer than a hundred pages. Likewise, the earlier part of his aesthetic project can be best summarized in the title of his seventh poetry book, a selection of his poems through 1994: *Putting Description in Order*. The result is an unfolding of catalog and sequence, an architecture all his own. This preoccupation with memory and witness has led the poet to the multiplicities of mediums and senses to which his language can give birth: portrait, sculpture, carving, photo, graphic, hymn, song, each in its space or counterspace, swimming in sequence or series, in colorful frescoes and narrative thread.

A few years ago I came across what would eventually make up half of Ghassan Zaqtan's tenth and most recent poetry collection, *Like a Straw Bird It Follows Me*, in *Al-Karmel*, the international quarterly literary journal Mahmoud Darwish edited for more than two decades. In two issues of the same year, Darwish published Zaqtan's long poem "Alone and the River before Me," and his entire sequence poem "Pre-texts." Darwish so admired the long poem's differential, its aesthetic variables, that he suggested its title. I was so taken by the long poem that I still remember clearly the sense of having encountered one of the finest poems I have read: its private and collective enunciation, versatile diction, adjacency of classical and modern aesthetics, narrative and lyric, its insistence on dispelling dimensions of time and place in search of new language where what is learned is constantly destabilized.

There are many out there who feel strongly that Ghassan Zaqtan is the most important Palestinian poet writing today. Among them are his contemporary the Jordanian poet and novelist Amjad Nasser, who is a significant presence in Arabic letters, the Syrian critic Subhi Hadidi, and Mahmoud Darwish himself, as he stated in an interview a few years before he died. Yet this testimony and those who gave it are far from the clichéd conversation of inheritance per se. In ascribing significance to Zaqtan's poetics one is not necessarily trying to establish a parallel national literary lineage—in the Irish or Polish manners, for example—where a poetry, justly and otherwise, is reconstructed into a narrative within the historical politics of the literary cosmos. Anyone who recognizes Ghassan Zaqtan's importance to Palestinian and Arabic poetry does so with a simple understanding of artistic innovation on a path of nonlinear continuity and trajectory. A Palestinian has come to ask us questions of the deterritorialized existence.

The need to explain a personal and a collective biography of the Palestinian poet and his/her poetry, while a necessity not particular to the Palestinian, is itself a quandary. Ghassan Zaqtan has his Odyssey, a common thread among all Palestinians, singular in each instance. One is tempted to register those personal details of loss, distance, and absence, and what they signify, especially in a preface to a literary work in translation. This would necessitate, among other things, a brief narrative of the poet's life: where he was born (in which Palestine); what displacement, dispossession, or expulsion he and his family have suffered; what activism and what resistance; was he ever jailed, why and by whom, and so on. Ghassan Zaqtan was born in 1954 in Beit Jala after his family was driven out of Zakariyya by Zionist forces in 1948. He eventually moved to Jordan, obtained a degree in physical education, and moved to Beirut and then Damascus and Tunis, before returning to Palestine in 1994. He now resides in

Ramallah. His parents and grandparents are deceased. Their death in and of itself constitutes an immense weight for the poet. His father, Khalil Zaqtan, was also a poet, and a committed activist who started the first school in Dheishe refugee camp near Beit Jala. Ghassan's son, Shadi, is a musician and a singer. Here is the end of Ghassan's poem "Khalil Zaqtan," from his 1988 collection *The Heroism of Things:*

> And I will gather the house of your chucked absence.
> As if we were alone on earth
> . . . you die
> so I can fold the falcon's wings after its departure
> and believe the silence that remains.

In his eighth collection, *Luring the Mountain*, published in 1998, his aesthetic project came into full fruition. Everything he touched seemed to enact a séance. And indeed it is the spirited interlocution with the dead that is a mark of a remarkable poet who is able to see "in what the blind see / a sound in the garden" and enter the possibility of unwriting himself, no longer the poet who's compelled to "lean over seductive wisdom / pick it out of the commoners' death." He would achieve this unwriting more distinctly later in *Straw Bird*, but it can be argued that *Luring the Mountain* closed the book on a stage of Zaqtan's poetry and ushered in a more transformative approach to memory and elegy in the following two collections. Zaqtan's earlier poems seem almost haunted by the spirits of the dead. In *Luring the Mountain* he is constantly aware of his struggle with these ghosts, cognizant that it is "Not Yet" that he sheds this "presence" for another nature, even though he can sense he's on the cusp of it: "Whenever I say it's time I went / the songs I thought would never return arrive." It's as if loss in his poetry has finally broken off into islands that seem separate on the surface but are still connected underneath. In "The Islands," the poem from which his 1998 collection takes its title, the chore is that of a rower, luring a mountain to stay distant, to drift closer, a here and there at once.

Zaqtan's ninth collection in 2003, *Biography in Charcoal*, negotiates memory and the sudden nonarrival of it in the midst of violence and war after the eruption of the Second Intifada in Palestine in 2001, a recurrent apparition of absence and dispossession. The poems in *Biography* confront what confronts them, including the human, humanized enemy, who "resembles the dead Arabs here." Though if Zaqtan's ghosts persist to "swim like black horses" in his sleep, he is able to enunciate the will to alter them: "Whenever I fall asleep / a horse comes to graze my dreams." But what really seals this conversion, this exit in the face of ongoing destruction, is his convergence on his own biography, his own chronology. The dated poems in this collection are not trapped in a binary mode of truth and document, triumph and defeat, the heroic and tragic, action and resignation, storyline and moral. Charcoal and what is charred push the limits of expression and form, and pressure them toward new lines of flight:

> Then the sound sculpts me until I disappear
> in order for those who saw to remember me.
>
> Thus the singer
> and the song
> are alike.

Zaqtan's chronologies of personal history are at their best when they simply "water time," host life and language. When we wander into, or with, Ghassan Zaqtan's Odyssey, we encounter his still, quiet photographs ("Four Sisters from Zakariyya"), his gestures of paradoxical calm that search "like the mad / for a gap in silence." We also engage his complex and brilliant knack for catalog and depiction, where the logic of clarity occasionally gives way under the additive weight of detail. In "Amman 1966" he neatly places the objects of memory behind a window, or in an ornate handheld basket that laughs at him as he weaves it, and he is caught not really knowing what to do with these objects, where to take them, or how to hold them: "My appointment is astray / and my waiting is shadows." In this poem, as in many others, his propensity for syntactical ambiguity, absent verbs (or incomplete actions), resembles skipped, irregular contractions on an electric heart tracing without necessarily missing a beat. Here's a stanza from an earlier poem, "Additions to the Past," in *Luring the Mountain*:

> The closet's corner through the door's opening,
> and the door, when the hymns swim gathered like handkerchiefs
> in the darkness of the plains,
> the air's shadow and the novel,
> the one she didn't return to the shelf, or can't remember
> if she did or not, its protagonists
> fall to the ground dead
> and she sweeps them one
>> by one
> with broom, reproach, and supplication

One is swept into his spiraling registry without being given much chance to fuss about purpose. His proliferative series are more than a database of memory, more than an economy of desire or longing. In another wonderful poem, in *Straw Bird*, "As If He Were She," Zaqtan's whirling inventory takes on narrative energy. Many might be seduced by its sense of mystery, but it is the process of sprouting and branching accrual that is magnificent. The poem is one of Zaqtan's many instances of becoming other, although we are not certain who and what. In fact, Zaqtan gives us a heads-up at the beginning of it:

> Something wrong happened there at the starting line
> a minor error that accumulates its dark with the patience
> and perseverance of the dead.

And the following corrective measures through a progressive series of "or"s only intensifies this metamorphosis of he-she, she-he to the point of indistinguishability:

> Or
> when the officer, picking his teeth, singled him out just like that
> during the midnight patrol
>
> . . . .
>
> Or the scent
> the scent that wakes him in the mornings, winter mornings,
> with a pair of Asian eyes that encircle him like a spring
>
> . . . .
>
> Or
> when he saw himself on the opposite lakeshore, wearing
> a light blue silk dress, while a few women laughed in the thicket.

Or it is, as Zaqtan says in "Cavafy's Builders,"

> the probability of improvisation
> the tenderness of verbs
> and the solidity of narration

to which we grow addicted and full of return: the known and unknown form the commissure for memory and forgetting, desire and reflex, an implosion within the simultaneously expanding mind.

No doubt Zaqtan's contemporaneity is well informed by a deep knowledge of classical Arabic literature. The long poem in *Straw Bird*, "Alone and the River before Me" echoes the fantastic primer to the genre of collected short stories, known as *al-Maqamat*, dating back to the tenth and eleventh centuries, specifically to al-Hamadhani's and al-Hariri's masterpieces of the same title, where narrative coherence is held within helical lyric, folkloric imagination, the prosaic and realist, adorned by a scattering of poetic lines. In Zaqtan's hands, this becomes a mosaic or chimeric architecture that bridges the past to the future, the archaic to the genetic, and the continuum to the quantum. And in this peripatetic spinning, time is not linear or circular but porous and full of truncations and offshoots.

Similarly, "Pretexts" forges its own narrative, as a series of juxtapositions that insists on a taxonomy of description. By the time Zaqtan reaches his *Straw Bird*, loss, violence, and absence are not visible in his rearview mirror; they have become "Pretexts" that mingle blithe lyrics and frivolity with folktales and ars poetica. In an imaginative sense, this gathers the abovementioned modes in *al-Maqamat* into the modern art of the sequence poem. "Pretexts" exploits loss in order for song "to spin us like two straw birds," a playful fragility to "open a door / and close another shut." He has left his elegy behind. He has "no reason to nurture funerals as others do." The process of catalog extends a ladder to the poet up and down the rank of pretexts for love and romantic antics with body and language, not land and nation per se. And "the signs," although

> there
> abandoned on the paths
> scrutinized by the ignorant,

become loose threads that hop, leap, and lead us to where "the signifier and the signified get lost."

This desire and design to move past traditional representation is a coup not only at the individual level for the poet but also at the collective level for the Palestinian who is still bound or defined through historical dates and expressions such as 1948, Nakba, 1967, PLO, occupation, settlements, refugees, right of return, and the like. In a mischievous or satiric manner, Zaqtan says:

> What I know
> and what I will know
> bore me.

He proceeds to wander

> behind the narrative . . .
> along with those who have returned from the heart of the text
> where houses don't take them to the stranger evening
> and roads don't carry them to the friendly suburbs.

A double nonarrival that is hard to miss.

The title piece ("The Bird Follows Me") comes as a canary in a coal mine. His straw bird is a construction collage, a folder of lyrical preludes he couldn't, for the longest time, unfold or "retrieve from muttering." Actually, this bird had already announced its becoming in *Biography* when in "Black Horses" Zaqtan mentions, among the things entrapped and piling up within him, "poem beginnings that flap like wings in my head." These preludes or poem beginnings have a significant, even revolutionary, impact on the poet's mind. For years they never took off: they defied incorporation into familiar poems. Yet they didn't go away or disappear. They were the "Not Yet" all along that Zaqtan sensed but could not command or submit to. And now they have become free to turn themselves into whatever fragility they choose: interludes, organs, and poem endings that are scattered about the body of his *Straw Bird*. The closing piece, "Everything as It Was," highlights this well:

What led him over there
in such cold weather?
Not longing or curiosity
but maybe fear or perhaps it was
the chill in the room,
though everything appeared as it was,
as he wrote in an old poem he could not finish.

Just as Zaqtan does not know or want to know what to do with memory and its accumulations in *Biography*, he shifts this uncertainty in *Straw Bird* to the body of the poem: he does not know or want to know "where the poem is, in its painful incompleteness." Instead, he is interested in moving vectors, his beginnings and endings released into orbits. Just when stasis seems to loom again, movement ensues, twisting and turning, toward the barrier, the limit:

he thought this kind of trickery
would befit the ending!

He could replace the "grandmother" with the "mother"
and observe
the disintegrating plaster above the door's awning
the upside down chair
where the mallow flowers stumble and recover
without being nursed
and the gentle light through the back window
remains in its same old place

Only the jasmine continued its climb, its eyes on the ceiling.

All the shifts in Ghassan Zaqtan's poetry—between memory and time, representation and transformation, elegy and praise, documentary and becoming—seem to have one central catalyst in common: recurrent doubt. It's as if his return visits to past, present, and future repeatedly end up in erasure, or rewriting, rather than in confirmation. In "Remembering Sleep" (the last of the "Pretexts"), Zaqtan displays the acme of his hesitation. His questioning and unanswering heart's major concern is how to swindle itself:

> Her effigy is by the edge of sleep
>
> and besides this my only trick is that the land
> be seen or returned to its people
> and that I shall think like a falcon . . .
> or have I been saying this for twenty years,
> give or take, and here I am still
> in the place still running
> free and mortgaged by presence!

Is this the same falcon whose wings he's been trying to "fold" as he said in the poem to his father in 1988? Actually, it doesn't matter to Ghassan that much. He is now more concerned with the paradox of "still running," of simultaneous movement and immobility. And this transports us deeper into one of his art's essential forces. To read Zaqtan's poetry is to enter and exit through many portals that cannot be fully listed. The potential for discovery seems boundless, even for the poet himself.

Of these portals, the most noticeable is Ghassan Zaqtan's "two wolves" that we keep encountering throughout *Biography* and *Straw Bird*. One wolf emits the chatter of running rhythms, and the other displays the silence of an ascetic freeze (frieze), two indefinite states of dynamism and inertia. Like horses, or passageways, for example, the wolf roams the body of Zaqtan's poems in numerous capacities that don't add up to discernible sign or simple duality, making a cameo here and playing the lead role there, and at times the wolf is simply behind the camera. The wolf is poet, banished, bandit, lover, guide, companion, predator, prey, earth, nature, squatter, sprinter, deterritorializer, reterritorialzer, and also "unconcerned when awakened by the watchman of wishes."

Ghassan Zaqtan's poems, in their constant unfolding, invite us to enter them, exit them, map and unmap them, code and decode them, fill them up and empty them, with the living and nonliving, the animate and inanimate, toward a true freedom.

Fady Joudah

ACKNOWLEDGMENTS

Antioch Review: "Everything as It Was."

Beloit Poetry Journal: "A Picture of the House in Beit Jala," "As If He Were She."

Calalloo: "Black Horses," "Ramallah 2000."

Denver Quarterly: "The Song of the First Patrol," "Biography in Charcoal," "A Carving."

Kenyon Review: "Like a Dream at Noon"

Massachusetts Review: "Beirut, August 1982"

Modern Poetry in Translation (UK): "Alone and the River before Me."

Narrative: "Remembering the Grandmother," "Remembering the Lonely," "Remembering the Repentant," "The Orchard Song," "Song of the Orchard's Watchman," "Song of the Orchard's Watchman and His Son," "Remembering Fatima," "The Absentee's Song."

New American Writing: "Islands," "Salty Hills," "A Horse."

Pleiades: "The Springs," "Silent Nature."

Ploughshares: "Wolves."

PN Review (UK): "Just a Song," "Wolves, Also," "The Springs," "Silent Nature."

Poetry International: "Song of the Drowned," "Cavafy's Builders."

Triquarterly Review: "A Graphic 1995," "Preliminary Sketch," "The Camp Prostitute," "The One You Accidentally Found in the Mirror"

Two Lines: "Like One Who Waits for Me," "Wolves, Also" (online), "He Thought Long of Going Back There."

The Wolf: "Wood Carving," "You're Not Alone in the Wilderness."

from Luring the Mountain

THE DEAD IN THE GARDEN

Don't open the window
don't wake up
I beg you don't wake up . . .
they were dancing on the garden grass
as if they were the garden's motive
or its meditation
and they were screaming there

Beneath the light
their dust was coming apart

it had rained at night
all night.

NEIGHBORING SOUNDS

Yesterday I became aware of some cheerful steps
before I heard a "besmala"
whose dust was weeping.

I had just seen a woman
who was alight for a moment and then vanished . . .
but her coat lingered in the shadows.

I heard a music from the neighboring basement,
a string instrument falling and withering,
and a wrecked laugh that had arrived from the tunnels
under the house, a laugh whose yarn
time surrounds and whose swerve
is led by some damp metal.

And I saw in what the blind see
a sound in the garden,
its form
and breath,
before I woke up alone . . .
some murmur sprang from the walls
and resembled the air
as it says to you: Here . . . here

or the air saying to you: Here

                                                    here

Who's in the city besides us?

ADDITIONS TO THE PAST

The letters are in the widow's room
in the straw basket
on the bed that is purged from sleep,
and within the will to fast, a will that permeates the corridor's air

The vegetables that are usually bought in the mornings,
the tickets, Thursday's bus at dawn,
the pillows
candles
and the patience where a prayer is pampered in a carving

The closet's corner through the door's opening,
and the door, when the hymns swim gathered like handkerchiefs
in the darkness of the plains,
the air's shadow and the novel,
the one she didn't return to the shelf, or can't remember
if she did or not, its protagonists
fall to the ground dead
and she sweeps them one
                    by one
with broom, reproach, and supplication

The letters that have not been opened yet
and the dead
return through the door's opening to steal
the bud vase
the orange sheets
and blankets.

LIKE ONE WHO WAITS FOR ME

When I remember him standing
under a soft light
like one who waits for me to remember him,
when our ghosts
slowly descend from the ladder
of the night slow-
ly descend,
after the evening prayers, the rosary
and the late night prayers
and the sleep in the paradise
of those who return . . .
like one who waits for me to tell me:
We are in the tent together
the one pitched for the fortieth day
of the dead . . . together!
Or maybe so I can tell him:
O father
no one prays for us in these corners
we have no narrators in the books
and no followers!

NOT YET

Whenever I say it's time I went
and got ready to leave
all the faces I nearly forgot
call to me and the houses
I stayed at and leaned
my head against their brick
or corridor walls come . . .
and out of their waters
where to the end of endlessness
the rooms crawl I was called.

Whenever I say it's time I went
the songs I thought would never return arrive
and the old hands knock on my door
hands that thought of me
or shepherded my roads
in a time that was . . . obliterated.

The same hands that cuffed my wrists
and gripped my collar
and woke me from sleep
dead
     and living
at the door O my master
O Mohammad!

A REGRETFUL YOUNG JAHEER MAN

I must leave this town
there is no sun for me here
no shadow
no state that delights the soul
or a rendezvous in the gist of speech

I must leave it sneak out of it
without sadness over its bitter heart

I have no business in the celebration of roosters
I have no bench in the garden
and no desire to sit

the birds have bought my journey.

I have no fear
no wall
and no horse.

I must leave quickly
and toss its laws to the wolves
its wisdom to sand
and leave at night
        as when I arrived back when
        no gray glistened in my parted hair,
        and free and nervous like a strange plant
        I stood at the gates

my steps were stronger then
my voice louder
my silence less.

The town's hearsay has exhausted me
its corrupt people
and reckless women
its saunter and illusions at evening
the senility of its elderly and the repentance of its weird folk

I must leave it . . . because
I want to remove the dust that has settled after me on the cypress.

I must do this while the shepherds are returning from their wells,
the lethargic sages from their holes in shadow,
the preachers from the night
where windows shriek at the sand

do it before they all panic and rush to their dreams
where the thread of desire loosens
the forbidden, the permissible.

And as they turn day over into night
which they usually do
I would have reached the edge of the plains
at the beginning of the cypress
behind the hills.

THE SONG OF THE DROWNED

At night I climb the cookie dough rope and the wooden carts
and call to my sister behind the reeds by the irrigation channels.

We sketch a school out of black ceramic
design numbers and dolls out of sugarcane

and a teacher stepping off the Jerusalem bus in the morning
angrily leaping into the market's mud
and boys, with their hair cut, mesmerized by the convent,
a bell on a white ram's neck,
and conquered trees under the sun
over the holiday swings.

The river was so fast when we were born
the reeds were thick by the river . . . by the marshes!

And beneath the mud
the drowned prepared fish for nets.

THE SONG OF THE BETRAYED

Midnight . . .
or after.

We were here
buying mysterious fruit
from invisible vendors.

A darkness passed through the cane fields.

The edge of night
folded the paved road,
all the houses were equal.
The screaming of glass ended.

The great air
ended.

Your heart now
is black.

THE SONG OF THE FIRST PATROL

And we were alone in the solitude of the house
while the house was dragging the light
which had been lost since noon among the pots.

Out of the three lonely trees
and the memory of the plains and the bells of the sleeping dead
a sound flew . . .
a woman in her thirties went through the door
called to her husband
while the light in her room was running.

Perhaps because the light
needs to find its way!

JUST A SONG

Thanks because the river flows
and the villages are fruits on the roads
and the roads are sleepwalking doors
and sleep is the shadow of death
its white land's first
and the dead are with me
strolling in front of my house
unarmed and peaceful
they posed for photos then left
singly
without an evening
or a calamity

and thanks to the evening.

THE HORSES' HYMN

The horses
the horses
that have stirred the dust in the valley's calm

The horses
the horses
that gallop split aside rows of date palms

The horses that drag the east
            by the scruff of the sand

The horses
the horses
in mirrors and hair
guarded by shadows

The horses
the horses
that cross the horizon
are etched on a crescent

The horses that released our kin
from the garments of smoke
then tossed their turbans in time

did not wait for us to say

The horses
the horses
the horses!

THE GAMBLER'S HYMN

No blame,
there's someone who loved
and whose boat
leaned this way and that.

No blame,
waves of garden failures
and contentment
and sleep,
shadow waves.

No blame,
we didn't go too far
as they did
and we didn't go,
we didn't pick the flowers of the dead
for the dead to enter
our slumber in the nude.

Something will resemble
our return to contemplate
the room of the past
the soul of the vase
just as
"the pigeons fly"
which is what the poet said
or
"the pigeons descend."

THE ISLANDS

1.

On the other shore
where island edges are
and where birds descend
abandoned like unmailed letters
there are men leaning over their ruined fates

2.

The vehicles come out of the shadows
also horses
soldiers
slave traders
and cages . . .
all this happens in silence

someone snapped the sounds out of the fabric
and left things busy with their chores

3.

Noon gathers
like a stabbed horse
while the poets lean over seductive wisdom
pick it out of the commoners' death

4.

There are no birds here . . .
water gnaws the rock's edge
while "they"
puncture the seashells with their teeth
and string necklaces
that accumulate behind them and push them
toward the edge . . .
and as the circle closes in on their wasting bodies
the threads are every which way
carrying shells, as "they"
bite the ribbed surface with their incisors . . .
each time they string two shells they hum
through their carious teeth,
some women the pirates will abandon
one day

5.

And as she climbed
I climbed
and from the top the mesmerized waving began its beyond . . .
the hill
the neighboring hill
the vanishing
then luring the mountain
after casting aside the birds
and waiting for the slopes
where the dust collects

6.

The only
remaining
ploy
now
is
silence

. . .

that's what he liked to say
while setting
aside
their taut pastorals

7.

White deities stretch out on his balcony
missing more than what white deities should be missing . . .
pampered and for some
concealed and distant reason, the matter
and the balcony
and the man sitting behind his novel seem old
and the musicians appear light
under the streetlamps

the woman in the phone booth is crying
someone is sending ghosts through the other end

8.

And while time returned alone on its feet
the captive decorative plant was
plowing the trees' shadows in front of the house
and climbing up the temple's steps . . .
time's black hooves fell and shook the altar
where the bull would arrive alone
without the wheat fields
or the prairies of paradise.

A GRAPHIC 1994

All this wasn't intended
wasn't clear
amid the suspicion
when we descended,
with merchants and dead and survivors and memorizers and divers
and wily characters of the night,
on some winding dirt paths.

The lightning that lit up the hills
sketched bending ghosts
and heads of anxious animals

behind
and above.

The glass windows let the night flow into the rooms
where now some other people breathe,
watch the belongings of strangers in silence
and remember their absence.

The dead who were late to start their walking
haven't arrived yet,
the carriages also,
as we were descending
shaking hands
leaning

while in the slopes children called out to their parents
in village accents.

All this
wasn't intended,
plotted.

A GRAPHIC 1995

The endings are not ours
not anyone's.

Endings belong to strangers
who weren't born on wagons,
people we find in the dust of corridors
and who happen in speech

people who are born from shadows
and unraveling mats.

And while we were plowing
they were laughing
and filling our pockets with dirt.

SALTY HILLS

The houses don't see us
or it seems as if they don't!
The trees don't bow when we pass
and we don't concern the birds.

Our desires are clear to slave and master
our fates are saddled
and our daughters scold us
whenever we think of the road.

We are the ones whom the states sent to you
with gold and books of the dead
we stayed in the alleys and bars
and declared our gifts to the point of fatigue
we hung silk over the junkyards
and with memory we shut the eyes of the dead
we have no king
and no judges.

The anthem leaves us alone
so we ascend salty hills
and like a file of dead men marching
we appear to the caravans.

We are many like affliction
few like content

that's how we became the soil of the story
and its mud.

Death follows our names
and fog mixes them with the mountain
and the shepherds shake their sticks at them
while our horses breathe in our sleep.

Only in the night
a woman calls out to her son Ismail:
Ismail
Isma iil!
Ismaiiiil!!

Then the mules quiver in junkyards
the hoopoes in cypress
the gazelles on slopes
the snakes in dead wells
and we rise as we have always risen.

What shall we do for your sake
when the horn is blown
for our sake?

What shall we do for your sake
when every time we fall asleep
we see someone other than you?

A PROPHECY

Since he has carried it
he's been lying.

The mountain is no longer upright
as in the narrative
and sleep is not enough to dream
where the dead walk about
like incomplete statues.

And no handshakes here
when pedestrians greet their shadows
and throw them a feast.

Yet
he has not learned the mirror's vigilance.

Since he has carried it on his shoulders
like bad news
he's been stumbling in his dreams
like one who's blind.

from Biography in Charcoal

BLACK HORSES

The enemy's dead think mercilessly of me in their eternal sleep
while ghosts take to the stairs and house corners
the ghosts that I picked off the road and gathered like necklaces
from others' necks and sins.

Sin goes to the neck . . . there I raise my ghosts, feed them
and they swim like black horses in my sleep.

With the energy of a dead person the last blues song rises
while I think of jealousy
the door is a slit open and breath enters through the cracks, the river's
respiration, the drunks
and the woman who wakes to her past in the public garden

    and when I fall asleep
  I find a horse grazing grass
      whenever I fall asleep
  a horse comes to graze my dreams.

On my desk in Ramallah there are unfinished letters and photos of old friends,
a poetry manuscript of a young man from Gaza, a sand hourglass,
and poem beginnings that flap like wings in my head.

I want to memorize you like that song in elementary school
the one I carry whole without errors
with my lisp and tilted head and dissonance . . .

the little feet that stomp the concrete ground with fervor
the open hands that bang on desks

All died in war, my friends and classmates . . .
and their little feet, their excited hands, remained
stomping the classroom floors, the dining tables and sidewalks,
the backs and shoulders of pedestrians . . .
wherever I go
I hear them
I see them.

WOLVES

The birds' departure from his heart
leaves the plains white
where the story is white
and sleep is white
and silence is the caller's icon.

A laugh of sand will sprout when the door is opened
from fear's angle, a hymn
for the grand winter, and the voices
of those who left long ago will jump like grasshoppers
when the door is opened.

Wait, wait a moment
for us to dry a moment
there's in our trace
a reckless lament
     and a ceramic bird . . .
and watch for the necklaces on the ceiling

Why don't you turn the lights on
or be happy with sitting

and watch for the fruits on the ground

Your voice in my room exhausts the silence
the silence of pots
the silence of shelves
the silence of writing
the silence of lighting
and the silence of survival
    which I have been gathering for years
    with the patience of one who's alone with the garden in summer
    or one who retrieves absence
the absence
that never stops.

WOLVES, ALSO

When it was close and had found its way . . .

the sound of its breathing
and the scent by the door told of it.

Someone's footsteps walked by
before it lunged.

. . . and everything here has disappeared
you and the others,
the distant clothes and those who were sitting
the few flowers in the pot
the color of wine
the poem:

The enemy comes to drink our tea at night
and leans his Tommy submachine on the wall

The poem
was it Darwish's
did he say: submachine or rifle?
The enemy's daughter was in the shadows
she had thick eyebrows . . . she had the taste of a slow river,
a voice sprinting out of sleep and a scent of leaving.

The visitors disappeared,
their seats under them disappeared in dense fog,
the actor in the death scene
before the end,

and the jazz song
in a club whose name is no longer clear
on a Saturday night in the heart of Memphis

the way coats looked while hanging behind the side door

and the wolves kept howling at me.

AN ENEMY COMES DOWN THE HILL

When he comes down
or is seen coming down
when he reveals to us that he is coming down.

The waiting and silence

his entire lack
when he hearkens before the plants.

His caution when he comes down
like one postponed by a hush,
and by his being not "us"
and not "here"
death begins.

He bought a flower
nothing more, a flower
that has no vase and leaves no will.

From the hill, he can spot the military checkpoint, the paratroopers,
he can spot the squatters, the mountain edges, and the only road
where their feet will leave a print in the rocks, mud, and water.

Losses also will appear from the hill
abandoned without effort.

And the fragility in shadow,
the Jewish man with a long mustache
who resembles the dead Arabs here.

From the mountain edges, all the caves will appear peaceful
and the road will seem as it were.

While he was coming down
the caves continued to stare
and blink in the cold.

BIOGRAPHY IN CHARCOAL

He will resemble me the one who will say to her:
People have fallen asleep
and the horses have grown decrepit in their enemies.

He will resemble me the one who calls out to his family
so it can be said:
We heard a voice from the night
whose swings were of women's hair.

Then the sound sculpts me until I disappear
in order for those who saw to remember me.

Thus the singer
and the song
are alike.

FOUR SISTERS FROM ZAKARIYYA

Four sisters climb the mountain
alone
in black clothes.

Four sisters sigh in front of the grove.

Four sisters in the dark
reading soaked letters.

There was a train
behind the photo passing from Artouf.
There was a horse
carrying a girl from Zakariyya
whinnying in the slope behind the plains.

And the clouds were slowly passing
through the canyon.

Four sisters from Zakariyya
by the hill
alone
in black clothes.

THE CANYON

They're bizarre, these days of salt,
as if they belong to other than us!
And like a well-spun tragedy
that is now complete
they begin to breathe when we begin to remember.

The forgotten hills on the boredom of slopes
the mountains that exhale to the west
the parading carriages of those who were murdered
and the total faith of one who's dead.

The hands that appear out of the dark to tell you everything
the deep brotherhood that leads to no wisdom
the talk that's no longer suitable for high altitude.

These days of salt are bizarre
disparaged like some rotten crop
and lonely now in the pit.

And as we climb, because the matter requires it,
our dark skins
and our experiments in sleep
roll down behind us, abandoned, to no return
. . . long names and titles that stretch to eternity,
accents, also,
that betray a countryside no longer necessary

They're bizarre, these days of salt,
so bizarre, they're not even good to remember!

PRELIMINARY SKETCH

The talk that remained in the house, when we went out,
remained alone
and agitated
pacing its domains
like a stubborn wolf

The talk that remained on the bed
and between the chairs,
in the mutterings of the hallway,
on the oil painting
and in the dice:
whenever I'd come back from my office,
where I'd lose a new day and a tomorrow,
I used to see it searching
like the mad
for a gap in silence.

I'd watch it as it unintentionally killed off its offspring.

AMMAN 1966

The dogs that barked in Karameh when I fell ill
the men who came to call my dad
the women who flipped their coffee cups by the door
the clothes that turned cold on the laundry line
the dust that arrived yesterday
my mother and her laugh when she's serene around us
all my brothers
including the one who died, he came
and was behind the glass, laughing from the cold.

The last cup of tea before fasting
the many eyes in third grade
and the sun, the sun . . .
the set over the teacher's head during the endless chemistry class
and the convent, the convent . . .
the morning buses that had just got in from Jerusalem
my family's belongings as they climb the river valley up the mountains
toward Salt, their loads on their shoulders, they climb as time descends
and those baskets, those baskets
whose adornment I now finish up as they laugh
at what I'm about to do
or have done!
Where do I take them?
My appointment is astray
and my waiting is shadows.

BEIRUT, AUGUST 1982

I wish he hadn't died
the one who died in Wednesday's raid

he was limping down Nazlet el-Beir
a blond
like those who come from the rivers in northern Iraq

Patiently . . . like an "insane" mother
war was spinning her wool that summer
as it is now!

Some song on the radio begins: "O Beir"
and it fills the house
my father's house in Karameh
or maybe his house before that in Beit Jala
the one I never find when I visit there.

O what the songs didn't tell us!

A narrow street
in the poor suburbs of war
neglected by all
things save summer and fighter jets

while the young man from northern Iraq
who thought I was a Moroccan from the countryside

was limping in his death . . .
blond . . .
not made any fainter by the lighthouse
or the memories.

A CARVING

The one who will come
has come . . .
the one who held me, like an oracle,
    from my words
    from my gait

and I used to observe him from my black hideouts
    his walking toward them
    them toward him.

Like a deep carving he clarifies his secrets as he walks.

The one I used to run into on the roads of sleep
    and he'd scoop water from my laughter
    has come.

RAMALLAH 2000

She remembers, calmly, that journey
to the hills the Haddadin leveled with their surprise
and white children
who were left to loot the night's narrators and the hyena's paths,
and with a woman's fright
in her sleep amid thorns
and stones as she whispers her charm in sleep . . .
as if gold bracelets came out of Mecca
at dawn to wear her sweat-drenched wrists.

She recalls or remembers
roads and mills and water in rock holes
villages dangling around like bedouin necklaces
and a sky of pale ceramics
carpenters seeking trees
stonemasons split by the mountain's dreams
fruit pressers on the hills
and caravans of forgotten merchants encircling the ruins.

And she calmly remembers the sounds of sleep
the death of Christians
and boats with black masts
that have been crossing the plains since the beginning of time
slow sails
and the longing of the tower and the convent's bell
that walks among the people.

And when she's distracted, she sees with eyes closed . . .
that her Christians on the roads walk in the miracle as they were born
that the Hebrews at the gate are taken by the sound of the horn
and the Semitic Arabs on the towers, behind the wall, and underground
patiently
water time . . .

THE CAMP PROSTITUTE

The intentions of those heading to her house
could be touched by fingers
chaste and proud.

Those who are late in the fields
will find her near small shrubs
and by the five grassy house steps
with the bougainvillea by the entrance.

Her bracelets that jingle in their sleep like a mysterious mare
her undergarments that color their dreams
her breasts that are well visited like the path to the mill
and her motion sketched from the sink to the bed
like a popular folk song.

The still life on the wall
the sheets and the two pillows
the cheap perfume
the nails behind the door,
where their clothes leave their odor,
and the jasmine outside the window.

Her astonishing bends
and her silence where her labor stones her.

The intentions of those heading to her house,
the passersby and the knockers,
the students, employees, chickens,
vehicles, guards, dogs, carriers,
cats, vegetable vendors,
fathers and sons, anyone
with a scent after her cracked sleep
was there
behind the children
    behind the carriage
    and the coffin
pure on their way to intent.

A GOING

Leave us something
we'd be sad if you leave

Leave us, for example,
if you'd like,
your last photo by the door

our summer trip together

that scent of pine,
your words or your tobacco?

And don't go
alone
and whole
like a sword.

A HORSE

And whenever I fall asleep
I find a horse grazing grass

. . .

always
a horse comes to graze the grass

. . .

when I fall asleep.

Like a Straw Bird It Follows Me

Pretexts

REMEMBERING THE GRANDMOTHER

Pretexts come along with her absence
and with the waiting of boats between
noon and afternoon
when the light is deeply fissured
and the satisfied prisoners, our grandmothers
in the plains, comb the sleep of hills
then age in their fissured sleep

We haven't seen the sea
but we can be certain, after the rosary prayers,
it's behind the line of hills,
says the girl who sweeps the courtyard

When I remembered
. . . when we had come up to the lighthouse
you lit a fire and kept me warm.

REMEMBERING THE LONELY

The lonely women
who neither sell their appointments
nor buy their appointments
kindle a fire on the hill
where the wanderers are many
and the air's silence is tense

The lonely
walk in the shadow
a flock of cypress trees beyond the line of hills
like a flute sigh
or a trill

the only trill you might perceive here
mostly around evening

The lonely
the ones we neither love
nor rendezvous with
sent an envoy to explain matters
to passersby

and spoke at length.

REMEMBERING THE REPENTANT

And the repentant women
who return to the foyer from a neighboring jealousy
fatigued after a long morning and an afternoon
bathe their shoulders and mix
their few excuses with water

And as the garden performs in front of the evening
a new role
that takes her away from her ten querulous habits to where
song awaits:

They go,
as they
always go,
after they leave
some bread
on the pillow
and a candle
in a wish.

THE ORCHARD'S SONG

Dear daughter
when you go to pick the quince
don't wake me

I've been dead for a long time, as you know,
like an ancient summer I sleep on a cold stone,
the sun turns me to the right and to the left
and the birds peck my head

Light passed me to shadow
shadow to light

. . . and the languages and dialects of slaves
used to fill the night when I passed,
and their amulets held the memories
and dragged them as if a swarm of ants

The singers' tambourines were swimming like a raft
around the radiance
lifting me in a joyous air,
and I was by the orchard's edge, the quince orchard,
reading an ode, perhaps by the captive prince:

I wish you'd turn serene.

SONG OF THE ORCHARD'S WATCHMAN

Dear daughter
when you go to pick the quince
don't wake the orchard's watchman from his sleep

He's been dead for a long time, as you know,
the bones of little girls make his pillow,
his mattress is out of his dead wives' bracelets
and in his purse is his fugitive wife's head

Try to sing a little in front of the trees
so they may love you.
How sweet it was, your singing, on the night
of commemorating the Prophet's birth,
we were at the periphery of some place
two poor beings seeking sustenance,
and singing
used to spin us like two straw birds

The dervishes were throwing their bodies into the circles
water used to come out of stone
stone chased the summer down
summer was of the sun's making
and the sun was with its kin

This is how a self is taken!

SONG OF THE ORCHARD'S WATCHMAN AND HIS SON

Dear daughter
when you go to pick the quince
don't wake the orchard's watchman
or his son

his son's been dead for a long time

three bullets
bathe in his heart

three ghosts
were at his door at midnight

three women
sighed in his voice before he opened the door,
something that resembled love

or what follows it
or might
render the matter hackneyed like slander

So don't wake him
he's dead
by a bend in the story

The scent of the river pervades him

he stood by the shrubs and wished for a while
in order to remember.

REMEMBERING FATIMA

It was so clear, the singing of the Moroccans who were swimming
on the river's face before sunset, the women who leaned on the bridge
among their children and vegetable baskets and tombs of saints

Distant Rabat with its people where al-Andalus hides,
Rabat, whenever I say I shall leave its halls, I spread for my will a rug
as it also spreads a rug

O Fatima
if only you would lean my way
or remember me,
that was what the river sang,
my heart would quiver
and you'd make me happy
and the gazelle in the hills
would find its way . . .
but Fatima was only a song
released by boats
and dead women on the bridge
in the nights of Rabat.

THE ABSENTEE'S SONG

By morning travelers knocked on her door
but she didn't wake

By noon a bird stirred her
from a book but she didn't wake

And at night a girl came from the orchard
her hair was short
her sleeves filthy
her load of quince

She called out to her dead kin
for seven days
and seven nights
full in count

The girl who knocked on the door at night

was there
with short hair
filthy sleeves
and a crow's sound

The caw awakened
a woman in her thirties
from her death

who said to the little girl:
I gave birth to you in a dream,
you aren't real for us
to love you as we would
other girls, leave for twenty years
so we can love you
and wait for you,
and don't grow older in the fog
lest we die.

THE HOOPOES LEAD TO ME

Sitting here where the birds know me
and the hoopoes lead to me
and the tapping on tambourines intensifies
as the dawn
and inquirers turn heavy

Our daughter has not returned from picking the quince
the wolves called out to her

The signs were there
abandoned on the paths
scrutinized by the ignorant.

FOLLOW THE WELL

The signs are what sent me to this well
what woke me and guided
the birds the plants and the absent women to me

My ladder is my mark
pretexts are my rank
and the women who followed me at forenoon
noon and afternoon
woke their husbands then came back on the nightboat
like things entrusted

With her darkness as my guide I ascend the well
for the light to drink my face
and for me to touch the birds in her sleep

so tomorrow she can say:
We had barely begun to follow the dream
when we awakened!

And so that tomorrow I can remember
how we walked in the well's darkness
until together we arrived
then parted

And when we drank seven swigs of water
quenched our thirst and were about to
we choked.

THIS IS MY ONLY PROFESSION

. . . to come up with pretexts for her absence
and all that I can delve into and interpret for the evening
that I will reach by evening

to climb out of the well as I walk
in the levity of night

the sound of the mountains

the waiting of orchards

the choosing of an enemy

and to author a bend in the story
so we can prolong the evening
or make predictions
and matters bearable . . .

to break a wish
so we can see the horses fold the mountains
that the sea embroiders

satisfaction and disgruntlement

the affliction of Kuthair the lover

the wolf of Uhaimer the bandit

and the elegy of Malek
whose distant desert Bunge followed him to the cave
and called him back to life

and the violet in depiction
when we nurture funerals in poems
or take a woman, without permission,
from a spiral staircase to a room in metaphor

What I know
and what I will know
bore me

From my trench I spot the frightened and envy them
spot the regretful and guess about them,
this is my only profession
and secret

. . . and contemplating them through the smoke of bundles and suspicion,
elongating their names when calling

and strolling behind the narrative, after the public address,
along with those who have returned from the heart of the text
where houses don't take them to the stranger evening
and roads don't carry them to the friendly suburbs

This is my only profession
. . . and gathering their sleeves from the corners of their seats
like a cold I gather them.

THE BIRD FOLLOWS ME

In the year two thousand or a little before, there might have been
a prelude that inhabited me, it resembled summer
in the rooms of bachelors,
I used to spin it in my speech

like a pleasant gait on an edge of marble, or dusting it
from what the hooves of mules leave behind
as they climb the wadi

" . . . in my house
women give birth to rings
and disappear from the world beyond the door,
here's the paradise of the one I love
and the journey
of the one who saw . . ."

A prelude like other preludes
I didn't retrieve from muttering

Like a straw bird
it follows me.

PRETEXTS

No vessel for the lover but his longing
no other
guide
or book

And pretexts
if only you knew
open a door
and close another shut.

ONLY HER DREAM WILL TELL OF HER

And she leaves me like an old concern on the shelf of her days,
my neighbors are photos of other absentees,
their stare at the dust,
their examined lives as they're summoned
in a hurry then thrust aside

Near me on the shelf are the roaming dead
and the living who don't respond
or see the path to her crime

The only thing that will tell of her sleep in my bed
is her dream,
and the embrace that turns a heart blind . . .
there is no hardship on a path leveled by wolves.

WHAT SHE LOVED IS HERS AND WHAT I SAW IS MINE

What she loved is hers
what I saw is mine
others have what they glimpse of visions that please her
and the passerby
has a plan for a meeting place

She stayed here for as long as passion stayed
lightweight on her heart or barely there

She walked in her sleep and tossed
flowers to pilgrims

but didn't notice the sky that opened above her
"a rose like paint,"
and slept for a while, and whenever
she saw a sign believed it!

A SMALL HOSTEL IN GENOA

The sign was in the monastery's courtyard
a friendly café overlooked two strange streets in Genoa

It looked like we'd passed through here before

When we reached the hostel's entrance, this confusion was clear
in the owner's tone that is borrowed from death
or in his hand as it handed over the keys
or in the chain's rattle

Or in going to the edge of sound until we caught our breath
among the disorder of dining tables, coffee machine, people walking by,
the bickering at the bar, the chaos of unemployment
in the economy page, the sullen stoop of those who sat
by the window, the quarrel by the side door

the winter that intensified at midnight to make the matter
deeper than the scene in front of the made bed, in a hostel that came
from another time, so the two lovers can stay there
for one night or less.

REMEMBERING SILK

. . . the princess is in her sleep and the evening is by the windowsill

Her closet two arches down the hall is open and black
her ghosts are calm in the dresser chewing on the memory of silk

Her undergarments are white
her bedsheets are white
and the amulets are forgotten on the mirrors

And the house chores were also there
the clothes the doves used in summer
the oil scent
and the shuffle of her hands as they left a trace
in the soft fabric where the breast sprouts

Something of suspicion
over the honey in the sound

There is no hardship in distance
though it's a self-standing reason
to wait for the galaxy at home.

I HAVE A REASON OTHER THAN THIS

I have no reason to remain here
I have no reason to nurture funerals as others do
I have no reason to wait by the doorstep.

CAVAFY'S BUILDERS

I have a tune in the melody
with which I did not arrive
but it is my only gold
and means

It has the probability of improvisation
the tenderness of verbs
and the solidity of narration

As if secret builders Cavafy had awakened
were passing through the hills
and started digging by my pillow.

REMEMBERING WEEPING

The weeping in happiness and the weeping in weeping,
the weeping that isn't mine and the weeping in song

The weeping that wears, as it comes,
her necklace, the glare of her shoulders and chest,
the forested shirt, the white apron and slippers

The weeping that is still squatting near my sleep
like al-Farazdeq's wolf:

"I split my food for the two of us
to the light of fire or through the smoke."

REMEMBERING SLEEP

Her effigy is by the edge of sleep

and besides this my only trick is that the land
be seen or returned to its people
and that I shall think like a falcon . . .
or have I been saying this for twenty years,
give or take, and here I am still
in the place still running
free and mortgaged by presence!

Just as al-Buhturi chose to imprison the wolf within his driving rhythm

"He squatted and howled so I composed and agitated
'til he came a lightning followed by thunder"

To the light of two wolves
I doze off

then the garden
howls behind the glass

the fence howls

and the birds howl.

Alone and the River before Me

I have a suspicious heart, brother,
and a blind statue,
and the news that amateur refugees brought from Baghdad stunned me,
there's a lot they haven't seen yet
they were crossing the bridge by chance

Intentions are in the ports
befuddled as their owners left them,
incomplete as the murdered left them,
and where our friend, the one you know, pointed, we went
without a moan or groan

Our country is far
and intentions good

We left, as exiles leave, houses more beautiful than the roads
and women more faithful than passersby
we weren't discouraged and our will wasn't stolen

We dreamt, as residents dream, of roads more beautiful than the houses,
of women who'd furnish our bodies and alter our language,
though this took us to neither hill nor sea

An infantry marching out of some front appeared
we heard its drone but didn't see it, and with worn-out eyes
and cracked feet they shook off the mud over the marble
and dried their boots on the billboards of the "founding father"

We watched
as if we had seen nothing, heard nothing

And it was possible to remember their lustful dreams, chase ghosts
and touch the buttocks of women to be sure it was just a dream!

But there's no mercy for the dead in these cold corners
no reward for those who are in the know

there's only listening to the mountain where caves are born
and darkness grows like a carnivorous plant

The cry of birds at the bursting dawn didn't overtake us
we didn't stumble over the wisdom or obsessions of our predecessors
though what we saw is worth telling!

. . . and then
a bunch of slaves started climbing out of a hole, up the walls,
even if the doors were wide open,
they climbed down to the city, roamed its markets,
men and children were shouting in the dark
swatting at it with drums and dancing,
women undressing on the edge of an abyss to distract death
from their children
as one of the locals explained to us

We felt grateful for our exile and residence

and said to ourselves:
we are only marching exiles, our shadows don't trail us over the earth
and like textile workers we hold threads and spin them to weave memories
that pant behind us and follow our steps like bewildered dogs

Who are we that we should dislike what we don't know
or love what we have no business in!

Then a jealous boy appeared:
his jealousy remained glistening on the fence after he left
and it blocked the path of cats, pedestrians, and the scent of basil
after the amateur refugees, with the news from Baghdad, had gone

His jealousy leaned on the breasts of a young woman
who came out of the shadows and took off her veil, placed it
on the grass by the soldiers' boots
just as I was moving to another dream

All this would have been worthy of consideration and repetition
had a young philosopher from Ramallah not died at 4:16 that morning
surrounded by his students, admirers, and three friends (two men and a woman)
it would have been possible also to remember
and add other scattered things
so grief could appear and treason mature

Chief among them
Buddha's lilac statue

or the photograph of a house owner in his furnished living room
staring at us out of his conservative classical death

a father's hermetic contemplation
a complicity of sorts with the daughter
as he expires beneath the oxygen apparatus

a woman's voice as she conceals her infidelity
through the phone's ten thick layers

it would have been possible to document his death or to remember
other scattered things in another context, like his dead weight
or the white of his eyes resembling a final resurrection
before the sirens were lit

If only he did not stand a bit crooked from the world, as happened with Cavafy
whose poetry he did not concern himself with as he did other poets
. . .
I have a suspicious heart, brother
and my stance is whole
no one can guess the whirling in my head
and I no longer trust those night travelers!

I have a suspicious heart and my admirers are obstinate
and in the wadis
if you look closely are birds and hunters
who wear in the dark longing's smell
and its form

Hunters who have other motives in the light
other labyrinths,
and paths that make a hyena huff
and the signifier and the signified get lost

Among them:
wind-instrument blowers

wily attars in the markets

barefoot narrators behind the slaves

and pretentious mockers standing on their bank
where we were born
white from black fathers

There are among them more than enough to make me superfluous

As I mentioned
my guests are blind and dervishes
I describe them as they appeared
in secret
the way blessed and guarded narrators are born
with absent minds
though if they absently
died they'd notice

In meaning they have a jinn's rank
and its language
and in structure a paranoid's body
and levity

. . . and for some reason I can't quite recall now
he moved a little away, turned his back to me, stared at the river
and said: I have nothing left to give you except this:
and pointed to the water
then wiped my face with his hands

I became alert and imagined I was in a garden in Baghdad whose fence
I had passed by when I was a kid . . .
and there was in the dark a fishing boat
a soft paddle transmitting the scent of sparks from across the river,
and quiet sounds coming from al-Karkh,
as all this seemed to me like breathing:
what I don't see as it has gathered

I rose and looked around
and there I was alone and the river before me,
with two maidens in it, one black, the other white
and whenever I slept or was distracted he would come, sit before me,
talk to me and I would listen . . . then he'd wipe his hands
with my face and I'd awaken, transported from one land to another land
one time to another time

until I reached the Tigris bank that night where the two maidens were
and I realized the state I had been in, and longed for those I'd left behind

so I composed these lines for the occasion:

I raise your secret above all	reveal mine to jinn and man
I light a fire of jasmine	and chase a dream of fleeing fun
And gather behind you the crowd's shadow	a salaam of vanishing to the gone
In pleasure I have my allure	and in sleep I see the invisible
As if I were your radiance	and you my whirling spell
I play and spin the soul	of life as I a plaything seek
And loosen prophetic horses	and ride drunker than a drunk
So here I am before you	a triumph brought to the victor
You're all I have as I'm paraded	the pleased around his benefactor

I elevated him higher in my prayers and embellished his favors then remembered
what he had told me as he was bidding me farewell:

"As for that which you did not ask me about,
it's your secret, no one else's,
and it doesn't concern me,
I neither help you with it
nor release you from it"

and I had asked him about all things but this!

He had tutored me
when I was a kid,

I would repeat whatever he said
three times
before the rooster crowed,
I would listen
then repeat twice what he had said
and by the third time
I'd add to it my own.

The Stranger in His Icon

SABA AND HIJAZ

Two lovers of this concealed place
just lovers
and a solitary flute
and two water genies
halt the hale chat
and ascribe to
the spirit of metaphor
as if we had entered the flute
through a fold
between the absentminded saba
and the wayward hijaz.

WOOD CARVING

1

In the house of cactus
I finish what I started

2

a novel for death and the dead
and a chapter on bird matters

3

my house is my journey, the wind my door
and windows are what I saw

4

I lost my fortune
but kept my acumen

5

a blind man with sight by the falcon's nest sculpts
my solitude so I'd be loved by a variety of selections

6

I cajoled hyenas and besides myself
trusted no one

7

I left no land to return to
and kept no road to arrive

8

when I came to
in the house of cactus
I had a full name and golden hands

"and untethered to remembrance
I was."

THE STRANGER IN HIS ICON

Nature that has left me hopeless
became arid in the fields

my abandoned homes in others' memories and feats
and the girls on the pier
with ill-intent they wait for me

the wolf's dream in its wilderness
the hyena desiring me and its neighbor

the cypress I tallied
the roads I folded

become distant and similar
while I forget and remember

I, who exaggerated everything,

go as alone as my mother birthed me
and sit in my icon.

ANCIENT ALLEYWAYS

Aside from her fingers, she got no sleep
she was there suspended in remembrance
patching up her fingers' dreams in a dim light

while
one bell was crimping the path to her house
one patient bell ascending the hillside
of junkyard and convent

one bell was limping behind the fence
and the Muslim cemetery
and passing in the privacy of jinn and the sleeping dead
by the springs on the boulevard of birds

one bell for stranger women
for the few wishes and for summer
for old outfits and schoolbooks
and boys dead by attic doors

one bell ascending the hill behind the ancient time
behind the shrubs on the foot-slope
where old dogs are tucked in the story
and the houses are gathered in the patient air

one bell was calling her name as she was ascending
perhaps to see her initials in cursive
above the pine grove

STEPHANIE'S WINDOW

Death overlooks the house in Ain Musbah
like a balcony

The handkerchiefs on the house's hanging basil

The prayers that have come since dawn with people
did not climb the stairs

The doves' thoughts are on the fence
brass music is in the police station
and the twenty-year-old policeman
from Gaza complains to the busboy at the bakery:

It's been two years since I've knocked on my mother's window!

The praying folk take their time
while higher, behind the fig trees,
the Frenchwoman's window is blue

THE ONE YOU ACCIDENTALLY FOUND IN THE MIRROR

The one you accidentally found in the mirror
in its dark corner to be exact

was there alone thinking of you
befriending your solitude

The one, because you are in need of company no more,
you called out of his darkness and fed
with your hands

You used to call him and he'd come
point to him and he'd jump to his feet

and as soon as you'd turn your back he'd unload on you
his hyena stare before returning to his corner

Now you recall all this
since you must pass a long time here
staring at the mirror
at its dark corner to be exact

as he sits in your chair
feeds you with his own hands
and passes you some water
calls to you
and you come

A PICTURE OF THE HOUSE IN BEIT JALA

He has to return to shut that window,
it isn't entirely clear
whether this is what he must do,
things are no longer clear
since he lost them,
and it seems a hole somewhere within him
has opened up

Filling in the cracks has exhausted him,
mending the fences
wiping the glass
cleaning the edges
and watching the dust that seems, since he lost the things,
to lure his memories into hoax and ruse.
From here his childhood appears as if it were a trick!
Inspecting the doors has fully exhausted him,
the window latches
the condition of the plants
and wiping the dust
that has not ceased flowing
into the rooms, on the beds, sheets, pots
and on the picture frames on the walls

Since he lost them he stays with friends
who become fewer,
sleeps in their beds

that become narrower
while the dust gnaws at his memories "there"

. . . he must return to shut that window
the upper-story window which he often forgets
at the end of the stairway that leads to the roof

Since he lost them
he aimlessly walks
and the day's small
purposes are also no longer clear.

AS IF HE WERE SHE

He thought of that feeling
the one that resembles your carrying another's suitcase and narrative
throughout the whole journey
unaware
while your narrative dies at the starting line

and its signs and faces and carefully wrapped appointments
desiccate in waiting!

He also thought
he carried the narrative of a dead person
or one who never came

Something wrong happened there at the starting line
a minor error that accumulates its dark with the patience
and perseverance of the dead

He should have known
when the dead used to open up his dreams and enter them
with the deliberation and caution of those in the know,
dead he'd never met, or so he imagined it,
yet they persisted to enter in their vague forms

He should have known,
when he asked the woman he accidentally found on the balcony

watering her mallow about her name . . .
she was wearing a manly shirt he remembered he had bought
from a street vendor in summer, and house slippers . . .
and there was what betrayed her ancient and noble presence!

Or
when the officer, picking his teeth, singled him out just like that
during the midnight patrol, the one that was mercilessly annihilated
a few meters away from the sand barrier

Or the scent
the scent that wakes him in the mornings, winter mornings,
with a pair of Asian eyes that encircle him like a spring
and persist in sending colorful butterflies to his heart

Or
when he saw himself on the opposite lakeshore, wearing
a light blue silk dress while a few women laughed in the thicket . . .
there was also a woman, he could not discern her face, who kept
remembering him and sending a hazy confession of sins he almost
recognized . . . a stumbling, a fast handshake, a cold hand on his bare
shoulder . . . and a voice approaching from the corner or the light
in the neighboring apartment whose sole resident
had died a few weeks before

This is where the matter used to befuddle him and the grass elongate
until it would cover the laughter of the women in the thicket, and the scent

of mint and sugarcane roots would unite to separate
the place in its entirety from what surrounds it . . .
and that feeling would begin
to encircle him so that he'd find himself
alone with her memories, that woman,
as if he were she.

YOU'RE NOT ALONE IN THE WILDERNESS

In Jabal Najmeh, by the woods, the wizard will stop me
by a passage for boats with black masts
where the dead sit before dawn in black garments and straw masks,
a passage for the birds
where white fog swims and gates open in the brush
and where someone is talking down the slope
and bells are heard and the rustles of flapping wings

resemble the forest passing over the mountain and nicking the night!

. . . and peasants, fishermen and hunters, and awestruck soldiers, Moabite,
Assyrian, Kurd, Mamluk, Hebraic with claims
from Egypt, Egyptians on golden chariots, nations
from white islands, Persians with black turbans,
and idolater-philosophers bending the reeds
and Sufis seeking the root of ailment . . .

the flapping of wings drags the forest toward the edges of darkness!

In Jabal Najmeh, by the woods
where the absentee's prayer spreads piety's rugs
and the canyon is seen through to its limits,
the furrowed sea scent cautiously passes by
and the cracks are like a jinn's harvest
and the monks' pleas glisten
as I glimpse the ghosts of lepers sleeping on decrepit cypress

In Jabal Najmeh, by the woods,
I will hear a familiar old voice,
my father's voice throwing dice toward me

Or Malek's voice
as he tows a blond horse behind him in his elegy

Or the voice of Hussein Barghouthi
laid to rest beneath almond trees
as he instructed in the text

And my voice:
You're not alone in the wilderness!

The Orchard of Roman Olives

WHERE SHE USED TO STAND

Where, exactly, did she, his mother
used to stand

when he suddenly spotted her
in the long corridor to the kitchen in Ressayfeh
or perhaps it was Jabal Taj in east Amman?

She was telling him of the chill in her room
when she died.

THE SPRINGS

How could he do that, end
his pastoral poem with a collective anthem
as he had always planned?

How could he do it in that abandoned
house like a voice recording of someone dead?

Dark curtains aren't to his liking
and he almost trips on the fragility of silence
the silence that rushes toward him out of hidden springs

while the dead circle him without pity
their ambiguous forms and memories of dying

And the springs, incessantly, mail out their murky letters.

HE WASN'T SLEEPING

There's a helpless woman in his sleep
a recluse woman preoccupied with simple thoughts
and needless accessories

A woman who enters his room when he falls asleep
she stares at his heart
exactly there, his heart,
then takes a flower out of the vase
before he wakes to count the flowers missing one

Whenever he falls asleep he finds himself roving
in endless arches
and watercolor roads,
affixed to the intimate scent of a woman's absence
as if he were strolling
in the memories of the missing flowers

Today
at 5:30 A.M.
she stood behind the glass
and stared at his eyes

and he wasn't sleeping.

HE THOUGHT LONG OF GOING BACK THERE

He thought of going back there
where he had left her listening
in a blue shirt and short sleeves

There was a man crossing the street without looking
whereas his infidelities were behind him stumbling like a heap
of obese women, whereas he was going down the three steps
careful not to bump into the pampered flower pot

He thought long of going back
where he had left her listening
with honey eyes and a cloven heart

A few boys were swinging intensely
from the peach tree he has no memory of,
while he was trying, in vain, to discern the steps
and move the bougainvillea pot out of the way

When, suddenly, the bell rang
the ancient bell on the hill
the hill which, since that night, the bougainvillea has covered,
that night when the eleven brothers killed
their only sister.

THE ORCHARD OF ROMAN OLIVES

Behind the fence
and the junkyards
by the end of the crossroads
there were thirty Roman olive trees waiting
like an army of sibling nuns climbing
up to the convent
where the dirt paths
had been leveled by hardship
narrow paths
like a woolen rope
while the convent
at the end of the mountain
was a kite.

LIKE A DREAM AT NOON

He didn't think, not for a moment,
that the garden is exactly behind his room,
that a woman sleeps alone in the other apartment
each night she prepares a cold dinner for two
lights a candle
then dims the lights for sounds to creep into her bed
and sleep within the creases

She selects her visitor the way she selects a dream
or furnishes a desire:

The door is for the key
the steps are for the stranger's smell
as he accumulates in absence
the jasmine is the terrace of the past
the fence is the temperament of her breasts
the type of love
and the distant grass, and people in an excuse-filled world
where to each time a voice
and to each wish a wing

And he didn't think, not for a moment,
to open the window
where without waiting,
like a dream at noon,
the astonished flowers were above the apple trees!

SILENT NATURE

The endings
when the last stranger sleeps on the house steps
or when sleep overcomes him
and the garden gate enters the shadow
and the jasmine
that appointments have exhausted
finds shelter in a space on the dovetailed glass
a space the doves seek
and also the dust
of buses crossing the bridge

There is no cause for fear
be who you are, kindhearted, for the stranger to see you
and for the river to have a guide

No cause for fear,
the songs of passersby, which the wine drapes
and the horses drink, have passed
and left in their trace the wind
and the women who endure desertion,
ancient vehicles, the earth,
the death on the roads of others,
mornings and afternoons
and the inheritors

And those who pray
have exceeded the Prophet's extra prayers
they delight in the recluse mosque beneath the crescent
and nothing spreads fear
besides the evening
and a lover's desire to be kissed by a poet in metaphor

The endings
where women who come out of others' rooms
search our dreams
and suddenly, like a secret, release the breast scent into memories
and laugh in them as a saxophone
is alone with a stranger's dream
on the edge of sleep at the jazz club,
or when the women find, in the stranger's heart,
the house steps

He used to see in his final sleep the whole truth
as it squats patiently like a wolf
and he was unconcerned
when awakened by the watchman of wishes:

Time is up Sir!
you can go now without worry over the night
there is no cause for fear Sir
it's no longer possible for a stranger to die of love!

EVERYTHING AS IT WAS

What led him over there
in such cold weather?
Not longing or curiosity
but maybe fear or perhaps it was
the chill in the room,
though everything appeared as it was,
as he wrote in an old poem he could not finish

". . . Everything is still as it was
since we had gone out to war,
since childhood or before,
perhaps the sun of those years made the white curtains grow
fainter, and the pebbles
in the hallway became rounder
and shinier or the grass had grown longer
or dried up!

"The three mirrors are as they were
the sheets, the shelf
and the broom

"the family photo
the leather-bound Quran
the rosary of the deceased grandmother

"everything was as if nothing had changed.
Perhaps we
we who fell upon the war
from the school bell . . ."

That was in the summer of 1986 in Damascus, his mother was still alive then
and there was an opening somewhere in that poem, more like a hole that followed
him,
he'd hear it stumble behind him wherever he went, especially when toward the
anxious
endings in his dreams, and even there, they, the boys, would continue to stare at him
and send out their perplexing gestures, the boys who did not return after the
midnight
patrols, and the dead who went back to sit on the doorsteps of their houses

Now he feels a saunter in him through that opening,
without knowing exactly where it is,
and where the poem is, in its painful incompleteness

Dampened with patience
overtaken by haste
he thought this kind of trickery
would befit the ending!

He could replace the "grandmother" with the "mother"
and observe
the disintegrating plaster above the door's awning
the upside down chair

where the mallow flowers stumble and recover
without being nursed
and the gentle light through the back window
remains in its same old place

Only the jasmine continued its climb, its eyes on the ceiling.

NOTES

from *Luring the Mountain*

A Regretful Young Jaheer Man: The poem was written in 1997 in Birzeit, a Palestinian village that dates back to the Byzantine era and currently houses Birzeit University. Jaheer is an ancient class system in Canaanite society, the fourth of five classes, below the free public and above slaves. They are often outsiders who are hired laborers with minimal rights or temporary enslavement.

The Gambler's Hymn: "The poet" here is Mahmoud Darwish. "The pigeons fly / the pigeons descend" was written in 1984 and is one of his more famous love poems. The expression itself is the refrain of a Palestinian children game.

The Islands is for the Greek musician and composer Mikis Theodorakis.

from *Biography in Charcoal*

Wolves, Also: The Mahmoud Darwish poem mentioned in the text is "As He Draws Away," from the collection *Why Did You Leave the Horse Alone?* (Archipelago).

Four Sisters from Zakariyya: The poet's mother had three sisters. Zakariyya takes its name from the biblical prophet Zacharia, whose tomb is said to be there. Artouf is a nearby Palestinian village, now an industrial center in Israel. Occupants of both villages were forced to leave in 1948.

The nineteenth-century British consul in Jerusalem, James Finn, wrote in his book *Byeways in Palestine* that in 1849 Zakariyya was a "prosperous-looking village" where "the very paths were concealed by the exuberant grain, so that we had to trample for ourselves a way through it . . . through an ocean of wheat. How I longed to have with me some of the blasphemers of the Holy Land, who tell us that it is now a blighted and cursed land, and who quote scriptures amiss to show that this is a fulfillment of a prophecy."

Amman 1966: Karameh is a Palestinian Refugee camp in Jordan just east of the Jordan River. The camp was the second dislocation the poet's family underwent from their original home in Zakariyya in 1948. Salt is a Jordanian city in the highlands on the way from Jerusalem to Amman.

Beirut, August 1982: Nazlet el-Beir is a location that literally means "the path down to the well." See "Amman 1966" for Karameh. Beit Jala, a predominantly Christian community on the western edge of the West Bank, six miles south of Jerusalem, near Hebron, was the Zaqtan family's first refuge from Zakariyya after 1948.

Ramallah 2000: Haddadin is the family name of the original Christian founders of Ramallah in the sixteenth century.

A Going: The poem rewrites a famous classical Arabic poetry stanza in the seventh century, by the legendary Amr bin Ma'd Yakrib: "Those whom I love are gone / and I remain like a sword alone."

Like a Straw Bird It Follows Me

The Orchard's Song: "The captive prince" is Abu Firas al-Hamadani, a tenth-century poet and knight who was captured and imprisoned during the wars with the Byzantines and composed great poetry while in captivity.

This Is My Only Profession: In the original, Ghassan Zaqtan makes explicit literary references to three poets: "Kuthair's affliction / Uhaimer's wolf / Malek's elegy." Kuthair was a famous lover-poet who was literally spent by his unrequited love and who, like Qyss Laila and Jameel Bouthaina, became known by his beloved's name: Kuthair Azza. Uhaimer belonged to the school of bandit or outlaw poets, a tradition that flourished in the pre-Islamic era and persisted through the early days of Islam. "Uhaimer's wolf" refers to a few lines in which he declares that he prefers the company of a wolf to that of man. Malek's elegy is one of the most famous in classical Arabic letters. Malek ibn al-Raib became ill from a snake-bite while on a mission of conquest with the Muslim army in Khorasan in central Asia. The Bunge tree was so abundant in the wadi region from which Malek descended in the Arabian Peninsula that the whole wadi was named after the tree, Wadi al-Ghadha, or Bunge tree Wadi.

Remembering Weeping: Al-Farazdeq (641–730) was a famous Arab poet.

Remembering Sleep: Al-Buhturi (821–897), an important classical Arab poet, was born in Syria and lived in Baghdad.

6

Alone and the River before Me

Al-Karkh is one of the main districts of Baghdad; it comprises what is historically known as western Baghdad, as the district sits west of the Tigris.

The Stranger in His Icon

Saba and Hijaz are two maqams, scales, of Arabic music.

Stephanie's Window: Ain Musbah is a district of Ramallah.

You're Not Alone in the Wilderness: Jabal Najmeh (literally, Star Mountain) is a hill between Beir Zeit and Ramallah in Palestine, and it forms a narrow passageway that gathers surreal formations of fog. Malek ibn al-Raib, in his famous elegy (see "This Is My Only Profession"), mentions his blond horse as the only creature that would grieve his death. Hussein Barghouthi (1954–2002) is another important Palestinian literary critic and memoirist whose last book, *I'll Be among the Almond Trees,* constituted his own elegy.